# Citizen Science:
## How Anyone Can Contribute to Scientific Discovery

Kathryn Hulick

ReferencePoint Press

San Diego, CA

© 2020 ReferencePoint Press, Inc.
Printed in the United States

**For more information, contact:**
ReferencePoint Press, Inc.
PO Box 27779
San Diego, CA 92198
www.ReferencePointPress.com

LIBRARY OF CONGRESS CATALOGING-IN-PUBLICATION DATA

Name: Hulick, Kathryn, author.
Title: Citizen Science: How Anyone Can Contribute to Scientific Discovery/by Kathryn Hulick.
Description: San Diego, CA: ReferencePoint Press, Inc., 2020.
Includes bibliographical references and index.
 Identifiers: ISBN 9781682827369 (eBook) | ISBN 9781682827352 (hardback)
LCCN 2019018535
Subjects: LCSH: Science—juvenile literature.

# Contents

# Science for Everyone

Every once in a while on a clear night, a thin, faint band of light stretches across the night sky above Alberta, Canada, and other northern regions. Chris Ratzlaff, a software developer in Calgary, first noticed the light in 2014. As a hobby, he enjoyed watching the night sky for auroras. These are displays of colorful lights that sometimes appear in the night sky above extremely northern and southern regions of the earth. But this light didn't look like a normal aurora. What was it?

Ratzlaff shared photos of the light with a Facebook group called the Alberta Aurora Chasers. Others had seen the same light before. In photos it appeared purple, sometimes with green light beneath. In early 2016 a scientist told Ratzlaff that he didn't know what the strange light was. So Ratzlaff jokingly suggested they should call it Steve. (The name comes from a 2006 children's movie, *Over the Hedge*, in which a group of animals decide to name a mysterious hedge Steve.) The name stuck. By 2018 scientists had published several papers revealing that Steve was a type of skyglow that had been entirely unknown to science. Ratzlaff was excited to get credit on one paper. "It's so neat," he says, "everything I know is self-taught."[1]

## What Is Citizen Science?

Ratzlaff and his friends in the Alberta Aurora Chasers group are citizen scientists. A citizen scientist is a person without formal training who spends some of his or her free time contributing to scientific research and knowledge. Anyone, anywhere in the world, can be a citizen scientist, even young kids and teens. "The common thread that runs through citizen science is that everyday people, who are not trained scientists, can contribute to science and be directly involved, that they understand basic research questions and want to help scientists answer those questions,"[2] says Laura Germine, a researcher at Harvard Medical School.

Citizen science does for science what a democracy does for government. In a democracy ordinary people make their ideas and desires known through campaigns, rallies, and voting. All of society benefits from people's active participation in government. In citizen science, ordinary people contribute data and observations, adding to knowledge that benefits humankind.

People participate in citizen science in different ways. Many, like Ratzlaff, gather information that could be very useful to scientists. They may peer through telescopes, collect weather information, track wild animals, or take water or soil samples. They may also share data about their own bodies and health. They may do this as a hobby or as part of a project overseen by professional scientists. Germine, for instance, directs the website TestMyBrain, which enables people to participate in brain research and learn about themselves in the process. In other citizen science projects, volunteers help label, organize, or analyze data that has already been collected. Ordinary people may also design and carry out their own scientific studies and experiments. Sometimes, as happened with Ratzlaff, amateurs make a discovery that professional scientists have missed.

"The common thread that runs through citizen science is that everyday people, who are not trained scientists, can contribute to science and be directly involved."[2]

—Laura Germine, researcher at Harvard Medical School

Citizen science is not a new idea. Trained scientists have been working together with the general public on research projects for over a century. In 1835 William Whewell, an English scientist, got thousands of people in nine different countries and colonies to collect information about the tides, all following the exact same schedule. And in 1900 the National Audubon Society kicked off its annual Christmas bird count, which continues today. Every year, ordinary

*A new celestial phenomenon, discovered by citizen scientists, colors the night sky with splashes of purple and green. This type of skyglow, eventually given the name Steve, was previously unknown to science.*

people spend an entire day walking designated routes or watching bird feeders and writing down every single bird they see or hear. This has become the longest-running citizen science project.

## Connected and Empowered

Today it is easier than ever before for ordinary citizens to get involved in science. Cell phones and the Internet allow people to communicate and share information instantly across any distance. When Whewell coordinated tide measurements, the telegraph and telephone hadn't been invented yet. Recruiting volunteers and getting them all to follow the same exact schedule was a huge achievement. Today getting a large number of people to contribute to a single effort is so common that it has a name: crowdsourcing. This is a very important part of citizen science. When a scientist needs to collect or analyze a huge amount of data, he or she can turn to websites and social media to recruit volunteers. Then apps and other software help coach those volunteers through performing the task, often from the comfort of their own homes.

New technology also makes it easier for ordinary people to catch the attention of mainstream scientists. If someone has a big idea or makes an exciting observation, he or she can connect through social media or a university website with a scientist who is willing to listen. Social media also helps foster communities of hobbyists who enjoy watching and wondering about a specific aspect of their world, from outer space to spiders. In addition, communities of activists can come together to collect data about issues that concern them. Trained scientists have begun to pay attention to these communities or even participate in them, answering questions and offering encouragement. Ratzlaff's online community worked together with professional scientists to investigate the light named Steve. "The doors are opening up. The halls of science are not inaccessible," says Ratzlaff. "If you're passionate and you reach out to members of these [scientific] communities, they will respond."[3]

Citizen science is breaking down stereotypes about who scientists are and what they do. For much of Western history, scientific establishments were only open to wealthy white men. And in pop culture today, a scientist is typically pictured as a genius in a lab coat, laboring alone to make fabulous inventions or thrilling discoveries. But real scientists are regular people, of all ages, genders, races, nationalities, and backgrounds. And most inventions or discoveries require collaboration and the sharing of knowledge and ideas. "We can no longer ignore the fact that there are things that scientists will never ever be able to discover alone," says Caren Cooper, a professor at North Carolina State University and an advocate for citizen science. She continues, "Citizen science is a movement that is challenging us to rethink how knowledge is made, who makes it, where that happens, and who it serves."[4] Science isn't only the domain of the elite few who have spent decades earning advanced degrees. It is open to anyone and everyone who wonders about the world.

"Citizen science is a movement that is challenging us to rethink how knowledge is made, who makes it, where that happens, and who it serves."[4]

—Caren Cooper, North Carolina State University professor

# Unexpected Experts

Jon Larsen was working as a jazz musician in Norway when he began scooping up dirt and dust from rooftops and roadways. He sifted through thousands upon thousands of tiny grains, peering at the most promising specks under a microscope. He was hoping to find a micrometeorite. These tiny specks fall to Earth from outer space. Professional scientists thought it would be impossible to find them in cities. The problem is that they look very similar to dust specks from car exhaust, pavement, power tools, and other human activities. But Larsen was determined. In 2015, after six years of dirty, painstaking work, he found what he was looking for. "I finally identified one that was different from the rest,"[5] he says. Matthew Genge, a meteorite expert at Imperial College London, confirmed that Larsen had indeed found a dust speck from outer space. "He ended up making a discovery that professional scientists missed,"[6] Genge says. Now, Larsen is a guest researcher at the University of Oslo and has co-authored scientific papers. The space dust he and others gather will help scientists learn more about the universe.

## Leaving a Mark on History

Larsen's work eventually became part of mainstream science. But he started out as an amateur with a hobby. Believe it or not, he was scooping up and examining dust for fun. An ordinary person with no scientific degree or training who questions, observes, and records information about animals, plants, insects, rocks, or any other aspect of the world is a citizen scientist. Some people who start out this way eventually gain recognition as mainstream scientists.

For much of human history, there were no universities offering science degrees. Many early inventors, explorers, and scientists had no formal training. They investigated what interested them and gained expertise through their studies. William Herschel worked as a church organist and music teacher, but in his spare time he built his own telescopes and observed the night sky. In 1781 he discovered the planet Uranus. His sister, Caroline Herschel, often observed as well. She discovered at least eight new comets.

During the eighteenth and nineteenth centuries in Europe, scientific training was very exclusive. Women and people of lower classes were not admitted into most universities or scientific societies. Yet that didn't stop some people from pursuing science. Mary Anning grew up in a poor family in England during this time period. She had a knack for finding fossils and made a living selling what she uncovered. She also studied fossils and made important contributions to geology and paleontology. Michael Faraday also came from a poor family but taught himself physics and chemistry. In 1813 he managed to get a job as an assistant at the Royal Institution in London. Over the following decades, he made major discoveries about electricity and magnetism and invented the electric generator. He eventually worked his way up to become head of the Royal Institution.

Gregor Mendel is famous today as the founder of the field of genetics, which is the study of how offspring inherit characteristics from parents. He crossbred pea plants to figure out how traits such as color and shape get passed on to each new generation. He did this work as a monk at a monastery, since his farming family didn't have the money to send him to a university. Mendel published a paper with the results of his experiments in 1865, but mainstream science didn't discover and recognize his work until 1900, fifteen years after his death.

Hedy Lamarr didn't have any money problems—she was a Hollywood film star. She had no science training, but in her spare time, she invented things. During World War II she wanted to assist with the war effort. So she came up with the idea of guiding torpedoes toward a target with radio waves. To make it difficult

*A Norwegian musician set out to find micrometeorites—specks of space dust that fall to Earth. The dust specks he found will help scientists learn more about the universe. In this image, micrometeorites are seen through a scanning electron microscope.*

for enemies to interfere with the guidance, the signal would hop through different frequencies. She and her collaborator, Hollywood composer George Antheil, got a patent for the idea, which would later become known as spread spectrum. Today it allows communications technology such as Wi-Fi, Bluetooth, the Global Positioning System (GPS), and more to work without interference.

## Passion and Enthusiasm

Today passion and enthusiasm may lead an amateur to become an expert in just about any field, even without a formal scientific education. These amateurs educate themselves along the way, learning mainly from experience. When Jane Goodall first entered the jungle in Tanzania in 1960 to observe chimpanzees, she had no formal training in science, and her only work experience was as a secretary. "I didn't know the first thing about studying chimps so I had no idea what I would find. They had never been studied in the wild before," she says. "I wasn't interested in being a scientist. I wanted to learn about chimpanzees and write books about them, that was all."[7] She made groundbreaking discoveries, including the fact that chimpanzees use tools, and she eventually earned a PhD.

Sue Hendrickson never got a high school diploma but has received honorary degrees from several universities for her work in underwater archaeology and paleontology. As a diver, she has explored shipwrecks and recovered artifacts. As a paleontologist (a scientist who studies fossils), she found the world's largest and most complete fossil skeleton of a *Tyrannosaurus rex* in 1990. The skeleton was named Sue after her and is now a major attraction at the Field Museum of Natural History in Chicago. "I love the thrill when I find something new," says Hendrickson. "I'm like a 4-year-old on an egg hunt—I just want to find stuff; I don't care if it's underwater or on land. I'm addicted to looking for and finding things. That's my true passion in life."[8]

> "I didn't know the first thing about studying chimps. . . . I wasn't interested in being a scientist. I wanted to learn about chimpanzees and write books about them, that was all."[7]
>
> —Jane Goodall, primatologist

Richard Leakey is another adventurer who never got a formal education. He grew up in Kenya, where his parents worked as paleontologists. Leakey found his first fossil—a jawbone from an extinct giant pig—when he was just six years old. He dropped out of school at age sixteen but found work on paleontological expeditions. By the 1960s he was leading his own expeditions and became the director of the National Museum of Kenya. Over the following decades, his finds—including early human skulls

11

and a nearly complete human skeleton—contributed to scientists' understanding of human evolution. "I'd spent most of my life groveling in the sediments," Leakey says, "so I had a fairly good idea of how to go about finding these things."[9]

These three people came from different backgrounds and time periods, but they shared a passion for their chosen area of research and wound up making important contributions to science. However, this unconventional path from amateur to expert is not easy to tread. Goodall initially faced hostility from the scientific establishment for her unusual research methods. Amateurs often face difficulty in getting scientific institutions and journals to take their work seriously.

Theoretical physics, for example, delves into questions about the nature of the universe that many people enjoy thinking about. Some of these amateurs believe that they have discovered answers to difficult questions and send their work to scientists. "We certainly have a tendency not to pay attention," says Tom Rizzo of Stanford University. For most of the amateur theories, he says, "you don't have to look for very long before you see a mistake that a physics student wouldn't make."[10] Ideas from outside the mainstream are still welcome, but amateurs in theoretical physics or most other scientific disciplines will have to go to much greater lengths to prove themselves than someone with a degree from a reputable institution. While it's certainly possible for amateurs and citizen scientists to make important contributions, anyone interested in science as a career should pursue a formal education.

## From the Sky to the Earth

Some areas of scientific inquiry, however, are more open than others to the contributions of hobbyists and enthusiasts. In astronomy, amateurs regularly contribute to discoveries. The sky is vast, and no one knows exactly when or where a new and interesting event might occur. In addition, time on the world's largest telescopes is in high demand. Professionals have to wait in line for time to make observations. Meanwhile, anyone with access to

## What Does It Take to Be a Professional Scientist?

Most professional scientists must spend as much as ten years in school getting a PhD. During that time, they learn a great deal of technical knowledge. A formal education is still the most straightforward and accepted way to learn advanced math, physics, statistics, chemistry, biology, and many other subjects. A degree proves to others that a person has spent time and effort developing his or her skills. It also gives a graduate much easier access to jobs and other positions within colleges, universities, laboratories, research centers, and scientific organizations. So if someone has a desire to work full time in science, getting a formal education is the best path to pursue.

Thanks to the Internet, though, education is becoming less formal and more widely accessible. People can now study anything that interests them for free or for very little cost using videos and tutorials or by joining massive open online courses. This means that the world of professional science is becoming more accessible to anyone and everyone who wants to learn.

a backyard telescope may point it in the right direction at just the right time. For example, in 2011 ten-year-old Kathryn Aurora Gray of New Brunswick, Canada, became the youngest person to find a new supernova, which is an exploding star.

Some amateur astronomers have become quite well known for their work. David H. Levy is a science writer and amateur astronomer who has discovered more than twenty comets. In the early 1980s he began working together with the scientist Gene Shoemaker and Gene's wife, Carolyn. In 1993 the trio became famous for their discovery of Shoemaker-Levy 9, a comet on a collision course with the planet Jupiter. Astronomers around the world watched the collision the following year. Don Parker didn't look for new objects but became well-known for his drawings and photographs of Mars and other planets. He worked as a medical doctor but spent his nights watching planets as a member of the Association of Lunar & Planetary Observers. Even after he retired, he kept up with his observations. "We observe a lot and can detect things before the professionals have a chance. . . . It's a fun thing to do,"[11] he said before his death in 2015.

Amateurs also regularly contribute to the study of animals and plants. There are millions of species out there, and mainstream science hasn't had the time to study very many of them in depth. Dick Vane-Wright of the Natural History Museum in London is an entomologist, or a scientist who studies insects. He told science writer Sharman Apt Russell, "You could spend a week studying some obscure insect and you would then know more than anyone else on the planet. Our ignorance is profound."[12] This comment inspired Russell herself to spend an entire year tracking tiger beetles. This common insect species can be found around the world, yet much was unknown about its behavior and biology. She helped fill in some of the blanks.

Amateurs may even discover new species that scientists don't yet know about. Stuart Harris, an amateur photographer, suddenly became an amateur scientist as well when he snapped a picture of a brightly colored jumping spider sitting on a yellow leaf in Namadgi National Park in Australia. He posted the photo online. One of the commenters remarked that it looked like a new species, unknown to science. But Harris needed to capture a live specimen for scientists to confirm

"We observe a lot and can detect things before the professionals have a chance."[11]

—Don Parker, member of the Association of Lunar & Planetary Observers

"You could spend a week studying some obscure insect and you would then know more than anyone else on the planet. Our ignorance is profound."[12]

—Dick Vane-Wright, entomologist at the Natural History Museum in London

Maratus harrisi, *also known as a peacock spider, is named after the amateur photographer who first snapped a picture of it in a national park in Australia. Since that time, Stuart Harris has led other citizen scientists on spider-hunting expeditions.*

the discovery. After hundreds of hours searching, he finally found another one. The new species was named *Maratus harrisi* after Harris. "It certainly gave me a personal boost," says Harris. "It's high on the scale of things I've done in my life."[13] In fact, he went on to become an expert in jumping spiders. In 2017, while Harris was leading a group of citizen scientists on a spider-hunting expedition, a woman in the group found another new species.

## The Race for a Cure

Citizen scientists who spend their free time gazing at the stars or scanning the wilderness for insects mainly do it for fun. Passion, enjoyment, and curiosity are all excellent reasons to participate in

## The Scientific Method

Citizen scientists don't have any advanced degrees or official training in the fields they study. Despite this lack of a relevant education, they still have a responsibility to practice good science. If they want their work to add to human knowledge, then they must follow the scientific method and ensure proper controls for any experiments they conduct. The scientific method is a process for acquiring new knowledge. It begins when a person observes an interesting event in the world and asks questions about what he or she sees. Then the person comes up with ideas about how those questions might be answered. In science, an idea is called a hypothesis. A good hypothesis can be tested using experiments. If an idea isn't testable, then it can't be proved true or false and isn't helpful to science. In addition, a good scientist is not biased. He or she remains skeptical about whether a hypothesis is true or not until experiments have provided enough evidence one way or the other.

citizen science. But some amateur researchers have very different reasons for getting involved. A scary medical diagnosis drives some people to delve into science.

John Kanzius was a retired television engineer with no medical background and no college degree when he was diagnosed with leukemia in 2002. He responded by learning as much as he could about cancer and then working on a system that he hoped would treat the disease without the horrific side effects of chemotherapy. He had built radios from scratch as a young man and knew that radio waves could heat metal and also safely pass through the human body. His idea involves inserting tiny particles of metal into cancer cells, then using radio waves to heat the metal, killing the cancer cell without damaging any surrounding tissue. In his garage, Kanzius built a machine that could generate radio waves. Then, to test his idea, he injected bits of metal into hot dogs. He could heat the metal bits while the rest of the hot dog stayed cold. He reached out to Steven A. Curley, an oncologist at MD Anderson Cancer Center in Houston. Curley says that as he learned more about Kanzius's experiments, "it blew my mind. I started putting together research proposals."[14] Kanzius passed away in 2009. His work wasn't yet complete—he and Curley hadn't yet found a way to get the metal particles into cancer cells. But work on the innovative cancer treatment has continued.

Sharon Terry was a stay-at-home parent with a theology degree when she and her husband, who managed a construction company, found out their two kids both had a rare genetic disease. They rushed to learn as much as they could about the disorder, pseudoxanthoma elasticum (PXE), which may cause early aging, vision loss, skin rashes, and other symptoms. They also learned that there was no cure, and even worse, the medical community wasn't making a cooperative effort to understand the disease. "We realized that we would have to do work on this condition ourselves to find solutions for ourselves and others like us," says Terry. She and her husband went to incredible lengths in their research. They even wound up borrowing space at a Harvard lab and doing tests on DNA from people with the disease. Terry says that generous researchers helped train them on how to do these tests. Eventually, she and her husband found the gene responsible for PXE. They also established the Genetic Alliance, a network that supports those with rare diseases by connecting them to each other and making it easy for them to share data. "People should be partners in research,"[15] says Terry.

## The Young and the Old

The people who can be partners in research include kids and the elderly. Both groups have a lot to offer society, in spite of stereotypes to the contrary. Don Parker, the amateur astronomer, kept up with his observations long after he had stopped working. Al Larson didn't get involved in science until he retired from his job at a sawmill in 1978. He read an article about a decline in the bluebird population and learned that wooden nest boxes could help the birds. So he got wood scraps from the sawmill where he had worked and started building. Eventually, he began banding and tracking the birds as well, and he shared all of his data with the Cornell Lab of Ornithology's NestWatch program. In 2018, when he was ninety-six years old, he banded over nine hundred bluebirds.

Howard P. Howard, another elderly volunteer, also contributed during his retirement. He collected weather data for the Community Collaborative Rain, Hail & Snow Network (CoCoRaHS). This group recruits people to install weather-monitoring equipment such as rain gauges and to share data from these devices regularly. The data is used to predict the weather more accurately. In a letter thanking the group, Howard explains that citizen science is a fulfilling, satisfying hobby for many older people. He writes:

> I wanted to thank you for recognizing the effort [of] many of us old/ailing volunteers . . . for many of us the days of once being the boss, the superintendent, president, foreman [have passed] . . . and suddenly you are faced with retirement and/or ill health, it is a very scary part of life. But being able to be affiliated with CoCoRaHS gives one a chance to do something worthy and for that I'm grateful.[16]

Young kids and teens haven't had a chance yet to get a complete education, so school is expected to be their main focus. But an incomplete education doesn't prevent them from doing science. In fact, kids are natural observers and questioners. "Young people see the world differently than older people do,"[17] says Loree Griffin Burns, author of *Citizen Scientists: Be a Part of Scientific Discovery from Your Own Backyard*. Most kids have keen senses and an even keener desire to look at, touch, and explore everything. Volunteering for citizen science projects and events helps kids learn, gain work experience, and contribute to society at the same time.

# Citizen Science Is on the Rise

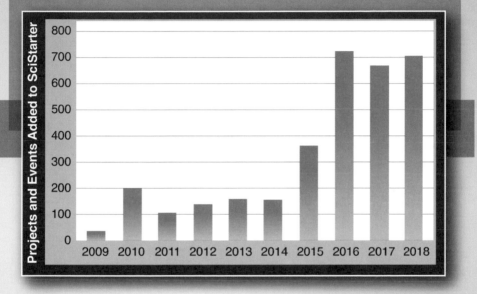

The website SciStarter provides easy access to thousands of citizen science projects and events. Over the past decade, the number of new projects and events added each year has been increasing. This demonstrates how popular citizen science has become, for researchers and for individuals.

Source: *Nature.* "No PhDs Needed: How Citizen Science Is Transforming Research," Aisling Irwin. October 23, 2018. www.nature.com.

Neuroscientist Beau Lotto of the University of London thought that kids have what it takes to do real science. So he worked with a group of elementary school students at Blackawton Primary School in the United Kingdom. He told them about his studies of bee behavior. The students then came up with their own questions about bees. They finally settled on one question to explore: whether bees might be able to solve puzzles. Lotto guided them through setting up and conducting their own experiments to explore the question. Then they wrote a research paper and got it published. Lotto's ten-year-old son, Misha, was one of the kids in the class. He says, "I thought science was just like math, really boring. But now I see that it's actually quite fun."[18]

Besides learning that science is fun, the kids also realized that no one is too young to make a discovery. Amy O'Toole, another student in the class, says of the research, "It showed me that anyone, and I mean anyone, has the potential to discover something new, and that a small question can lead into a big discovery."[19] This is the secret that citizen science hopes to bring out into the open. Anyone who asks a question about the world also has the means to seek an answer to that question. It doesn't matter who you are or what you know. You can always learn about the things you don't yet know. And you can most likely find experts willing to help you make your way closer to an answer.

# Gathering a Team

Every summer, monarch butterflies flutter through the countryside of Canada and the northern United States. But in the fall, they leave. Where do they go for the winter? Back in the 1950s no one knew the answer. Fred Urquhart, a zoologist at the University of Toronto in Canada, decided to find out. He developed a way to attach a tiny tag to a butterfly's wing. The tag identified the insect while still allowing it to fly normally. It also instructed anyone who found the insect to report it to Urquhart's university. He and his wife, Norah, spent countless hours tagging thousands of butterflies. But the couple came to realize this effort wouldn't be enough. To figure out where the butterflies spent the winter, they would need help. So they began recruiting volunteers.

By the 1970s hundreds of citizen scientists were helping tag and track monarch butterflies as part of the Insect Migration Association. The Urquharts marked all sightings of the insects on maps and realized most of the population was going into Mexico. Armed with that clue, they asked volunteers in Mexico for help. Kenneth Brugger and his wife, Cathy Aguado, (also known as Catalina Trail) responded. In 1975, with the help of locals, the couple located millions of monarchs clustered on tree trunks and branches in a mountain forest in central Mexico. The locals were curious about the monarchs' migration as well. They hadn't known where their butterflies went in the spring and summer. In 1976 the Urquharts visited the forest and found a butterfly bearing a familiar tag. A pair of Insect Migration Association volunteers, a teacher and his teenage student, had affixed the tag in Minnesota. Seeing it in Mexico was proof that the mystery had been solved.

At the time, scientists rarely reached out to the public for assistance in their research, and ordinary people had no idea that they could do anything to help solve scientific mysteries. The Urquharts came up with a brilliant and original way to map butterfly migration. As a bonus, their program increased the public's understanding of monarchs and enthusiasm for science.

## Stronger Together

While it is entirely possible for individual amateurs such as Gregor Mendel and Jane Goodall to make discoveries, citizen science becomes truly powerful when it brings many people together. All scientific research requires the collection of data. And in many cases that data must come from a very large population, a long time period, or a vast area. Learning about butterfly migration required data from hundreds of thousands of butterflies ranging over an entire continent. Learning about bird populations over time required bird counts each winter. And learning about tides in the Atlantic required collecting data at the same time from opposite sides of the ocean. In these cases and others like them, it was impossible for scientists working alone or even in small groups to gather enough data or the right kinds of data to accomplish their research goals.

Though the mystery of the monarch's migration pattern has been answered, there are plenty more unanswered questions about these butterflies. And scientists now realize that citizens can help find the answers. The Insect Migration Association became Monarch Watch, an organization that continues to recruit and train volunteers to tag monarchs. Volunteers with the organization also help protect monarch habitats and plant milkweed, the only plant monarch caterpillars can eat. Many other similar organizations and research projects have been created across numerous scientific fields to recruit citizen volunteers to assist in data collection.

Crowdsourcing is an essential part of these programs. First, trained scientists come up with an idea that requires the participation of volunteers. Then, the scientists use websites, social media, and apps to recruit and train volunteers and to coordinate their data-collection efforts. Scientists receive and analyze

*A volunteer tags a monarch butterfly at Quivira National Wildlife Refuge in Kansas. Thousands of citizen scientists, trained by the Monarch Watch group, have tagged monarchs to help researchers study their migration patterns and habits.*

the data. They typically share the results with the citizens who participated, and the scientists may credit citizen scientists in any papers that they publish in academic journals.

## From Birds to Bugs and Beyond

Monarch Watch is just one of numerous citizen science projects that ask volunteers to get out and observe insects, birds, frogs, fish, and more. The National Audubon Society continues to run annual Christmas bird counts, but that event only takes place in the United States. The Great Backyard Bird Count, launched in 1998 by the National Audubon Society and the Cornell Lab of Ornithology, invites people from anywhere in the world to record all the birds they see for at least fifteen minutes during a four-day

## Watch Out for Mistakes

Some worry about the quality of data that amateurs collect. People who lack training are more likely to make mistakes, such as misidentifying an animal, measuring amounts of rain or snow incorrectly, or failing to follow directions precisely. A 2017 study published in the *Bulletin of the Ecological Society of America* found that volunteers' work is often not very accurate compared to that of professionals. But when volunteers receive training or work on a project for a long time, accuracy improves. Plus, for some research projects, a large amount of possibly problematic data is better than a very small amount of excellent data. "Sheer numbers outweigh problems," says Doug Wesley, a meteorologist at the University of Colorado, Boulder, who has used citizen science data to analyze storms. "Would you rather have five perfect observations, or one hundred, of which eighty are good?" he asks. In addition, when enough people participate, researchers can build redundancy into the project. That means more than one person does the same measurement, effectively checking each other's work.

Quoted in Caren Cooper, *Citizen Science: How Ordinary People Are Changing the Face of Discovery*. New York: Overlook, 2016, p. 23.

period. In 2019 over two hundred thousand people from over one hundred different countries participated. "The Great Backyard Bird Count is a great way to introduce people to participation in community science,"[20] says Gary Langham, vice president of the National Audubon Society. He explains that the event provides a yearly snapshot of bird populations all around the world, which helps scientists understand how global events like climate change are affecting birds.

Other citizen science projects ask participants to record sightings of ants, bark beetles, hummingbirds, koalas, ladybugs, moths, and more. These projects usually seek to better understand the health and range of a population or the behavior of animals. For example, FrogWatch USA, a citizen science program run by the Association of Zoos and Aquariums, seeks to track population declines. Volunteers must join a local chapter and attend a training session to learn how to identify frogs by their calls. Then they commit to spending multiple evenings over a seven-month period sitting quietly at a wetlands site, recording all the frogs that they hear for three minutes. Project Squirrel, on the other hand, collects sightings to better understand squirrels and their behavior. It doesn't require any special training or long-term commitment. Volunteers simply fill out an online survey recording their squirrel observations from wherever they happen to be. The project welcomes contributions from anyone at any time—even if they see no squirrels.

These types of projects aren't limited to animals. Seagrass-Spotter is a project that invites citizens from anywhere in the world to submit photos and observations of sea grass through a website or app. The organizers point out that sea grass meadows support fish populations but are under threat from pollution and human activity. Observations from citizen scientists help track sea grass habitats and also raise awareness.

Some projects ask for more than just photos or sighting notes. The project Mastodon Matrix, which ended in 2018, enlisted volunteers, including classrooms of elementary school students, to help search through 22,000 pounds (9,979 kg) of dirt that had been excavated from around the remains of an ancient mastodon. Volunteers received their dirt in the mail along with instructions on how to look through it. Then they mailed any hairs, shells, fossils, or other interesting things back to the researchers.

Two other research projects collected material that most people would just toss in the trash. In 2016 and 2017 scientists at Northern Arizona University asked people to send in the bodies of ticks that had bitten them or their pets. The researchers analyzed these bodies to learn more about tick-borne diseases, and in exchange they provided donors with information about the ticks they sent in. Meanwhile, the Western Australia Department of Fisheries collects fish remains as part of a citizen science program called Send Us Your Skeletons. When recreational or professional fishers catch a fish, they fillet it, keeping only the meat. This program asks people to donate the rest of the fish—the head, skeleton, and guts. Scientists use the skeletons to determine the fishes' ages and to assess how fish populations are growing or declining.

## Getting People Out in Nature

Some citizen science programs aren't devoted to just one type of animal or plant. These accept sightings of anything from the natural world. They are mainly focused on education and getting people to explore the natural world. Project Noah, a platform backed by the National Geographic Society, offers an app and website that make it easy for people anywhere in the world to collect and share their observations of nature. The iNaturalist app provides a similar service. Users track their observations with maps, notes, and photos. People in the community, including some professional scientists and experts, help identify these sightings. Members Fred Melgert and Carla Hoegen have made over twenty thousand observations of over eight hundred species of desert flower since joining in 2018. "We started hiking and got interested in flowers along the way,"[21] their user profile reads. Though education is a primary goal of these platforms, they also help crowdsource data about ecology.

Some motivated people find citizen science platforms and projects on their own. But it often takes a special event to get new volunteers involved. The City Nature Challenge encourages people to document urban animal and plant life. The competition pits cities against each other to see which one can log the most participants, observations, and different species. A BioBlitz is another common event that anyone can organize through the iNaturalist platform. A BioBlitz brings people of all ages and levels of expertise together on an expedition into nature to identify as many species as possible. In 2013 seven-year-old Imani participated in a BioBlitz at the Jean Lafitte National Historical Park and Preserve outside of New Orleans, Louisiana. "I felt like an explorer and I felt like I could touch anything,"[22] she says.

## Watching the Weather

Large groups of citizen scientists collect data on all aspects of the environment, from animals and plants to water, air, and weather. CoCoRaHS has over twenty thousand volunteers gathering regular measurements of how much precipitation (rain, hail, or snow) falls at their homes. David Herring, a salesperson for the home health care industry, spends his spare time monitoring the weather for CoCoRaHS and training new volunteers. He says his morning routine is "start the coffee, feed the dogs, check the catch in the rain gauge."[23] He also measures temperature, humidity, barometric pressure, wind speed, and wind direction.

*A volunteer weather observer in Tennessee checks a rain gauge for measurements that he will send to the National Weather Service. He is a participant in the Community Collaborative Rain, Hail & Snow Network (CoCoRaHS).*

Weather stations and satellites use radar to constantly monitor and predict precipitation. So why do meteorologists need ordinary people to go out and collect data? Weather is an incredibly complex system. Severe rain and flooding could impact one town and not the next. Low-cost home rain gauges can provide much more specific, localized weather information than expensive weather satellites. Henry Reges, the national coordinator of CoCoRaHS, explains that more data is always better. "The more observers we have in a community, the clearer the picture of how much rain or snow fell where," he says. "It's just like the number of pixels in a photo, the more pixels, the better the image."[24]

"The more observers we have in a community, the clearer the picture of how much rain or snow fell where. It's just like the number of pixels in a photo, the more pixels, the better the image."[24]

—Henry Reges, national coordinator of CoCoRaHS

## Fighting Pollution

When it comes to the health of the environment as a whole, more data also helps paint a better picture. All around the world, a variety of projects engage citizens to collect and test air, water, and soil samples, looking for contaminants. Water testing helps experts monitor the quality of water resources. The EarthEcho Water Challenge kicks off each year on March 22, the United Nations World Water Day, and runs through December. Organizations or individuals that want to participate purchase water test kits and use them to measure several important characteristics in nearby bodies of water. People from over 140 different countries have participated in the testing.

Light and noise pollution are two lesser known environmental problems. Excess noise and light both waste energy and negatively impact some animals and plants. Citizen scientists help to monitor both issues. For example, Noise Tube is a project that addresses noise pollution. Participants download a mobile app

## Prison Science

People of all different careers and social situations may become citizen scientists. That includes prison inmates. Several organizations and research projects have made it possible for people in prison to assist with research. In the early 2000s, the Moss-in-Prisons project challenged inmates at Cedar Creek Corrections Center in Littlerock, Washington, to find new methods for growing large amounts of moss to replace plants that had been taken illegally from forests. "I need help from people who have long periods of time available to observe and measure the growing mosses; access to extensive space to lay out flats of plants; and fresh minds to put forward innovative solutions," says Nalini Nadkarni of Evergreen State College, who led the project. She got valuable information for her research, and the inmates gained valuable experience. One of her volunteers even went on to enroll in a PhD program after his release. Nadkarni went on to cofound the Sustainability in Prisons Project. As of 2018, among other projects, inmates at the Mission Creek Corrections Center for Women in Belfair, Washington, were participating in efforts to better understand and protect an endangered butterfly.

Quoted in National Science Foundation, "Inmates Conduct Ecological Research on Slow-Growing Mosses," October 17, 2008. www.nsf.gov.

and use it to record background noise in their neighborhoods. The Globe at Night project invites people from anywhere in the world to submit data on the brightness of the night sky during specified time periods. The main goal of the project is to raise awareness of light pollution, but scientists have used the data as well. For example, they have studied how light pollution levels affect bat behavior. To measure brightness, participants usually note how many stars they can see in a specific constellation. Over twelve years, people from 180 countries have participated in the project.

## The Miniature World of Microbes

Citizen science projects also enlist volunteers to gather data that could help lead to advances in medicine. Microbiology is an especially important area for citizen science. Microbes are organisms too small to see with the unaided eye, such as bacteria, viruses, and fungi. Some microbes, better known as germs, make people sick. Doctors can cure most bacterial infections with antibiotics. But some germs are learning to resist current antibiotics. Scientists are racing to find new ones.

One of the best places to look for new antibiotics is in dirt. The microbes that live there often produce chemicals to fight and kill each other. Some of those chemicals make effective antibiotics. Several citizen science programs, including Drugs from Dirt, What's in Your Backyard?, and Swab and Send, collect dirt or other microbial samples from volunteers. They then process those samples to look for new species of bacteria. And they aren't hard to find. "Every place you step, there's 10,000 bacteria, most of which we've never seen,"[25] says Sean Brady, a biochemist at Rockefeller University in New York who leads the Drugs from Dirt project. In 2018, after analyzing hundreds of soil samples, his team's work paid off. They extracted a new type of antibiotic from soil microbes. These programs are still accepting samples from volunteers as they look for more new antibiotics. "If I've got samples coming in from all over the world, that's quicker than me just going out and finding them, and the diversity is increased,"[26] says Adam Roberts, a microbiologist at the Liverpool School of Tropical Medicine in the United Kingdom, who leads the Swab and Send project.

"If I've got samples coming in from all over the world, that's quicker than me just going out and finding them, and the diversity is increased."[26]

—Adam Roberts, microbiologist at the Liverpool School of Tropical Medicine

Medical researchers are also investigating the potential for probiotic treatments. Developing an antibiotic is like creating a weapon of mass destruction. It kills all bacteria, good and bad. Developing probiotics, on the other hand, is like waging guerrilla warfare. Probiotic therapies would send in good bacteria to do battle with bad germs. However, probiotic treatments are not yet backed by solid research. To get to the point that these treatments are safe and dependable, scientists need to understand a lot more about the microbial world. Citizen scientists are helping add to this understanding. Your Wild Life is a group that leads citizen science projects, mainly to learn more about the biodiversity of microbes that live on and around people. Two of the group's past projects asked volunteers to gather microbes from their belly buttons and armpits. Currently, the group is collecting samples of microbes from showerheads and clothing. The goal of all of these projects is to better understand the types of microbes that live in each environment and whether a person's physical traits or lifestyle choices affect these populations.

The American Gut Project, founded in 2012, collects volunteers' lifestyle and medical history information as well as microbe samples from their tongues, hands, or feces. Researchers use the information to learn more about how factors such as diet and disease are connected to the microbiome, or the community of microbes living on and in people's bodies. For example, they've learned that people who eat many different types of plants have more diverse ecosystems of gut bacteria. Participants who choose to send in samples of their feces use a special kit to help them safely collect and send in the material. "It's really amazing that more than 10,000 people—members of the public who want to get involved in science whether or not they work in a lab or have a PhD—have mailed their poop to our lab so that we can find out what makes a difference in somebody's microbiome,"[27] says Rob Knight, a cofounder of the American Gut Project and director of the Center for Microbiome Innovation at the University of California, San Diego.

"It's really amazing that more than 10,000 people . . . have mailed their poop to our lab so that we can find out what makes a difference in somebody's microbiome."[27]

—Rob Knight, director of the Center for Microbiome Innovation at the University of California, San Diego

## Beyond Mere Research Subjects

Any researcher who studies human behavior, health, or cognition needs people to participate in experiments. In several unfortunate cases throughout history, people have been forced to become test subjects, but this goes against ethical standards in science. Subjects today participate voluntarily or receive some form of compensation. Either way, they are usually treated as passive participants in science. They take a survey, go through a test, or supply a sample, and that's the extent of their involvement.

A citizen science research project treats participants quite differently. The subjects get involved in the research in some way. For example, in the American Gut Project, all participants received a report explaining the microbes found in their sample. They could also choose to join an online forum, Gut Instinct, to talk with other participants about potential relationships between microbes and lifestyle. People love to learn about themselves, so sharing results with research subjects helps boost participation. Websites such as TestMyBrain and Volunteer Science offer numerous opportunities to participate in brief surveys or experiments that researchers in psychology, neuroscience, behavioral science, and other fields have put together. Participants usually get to see how their results compare to others who took the same test.

Researchers have to be very careful about sharing results, since it could lead to a breach of privacy. But when a citizen science research project is designed correctly, everyone benefits from open sharing of knowledge. The All of Us Research Program from the National Institutes of Health is an ambitious program aiming to collect personal information and health data—including health history and blood and urine samples—from 1 million volunteers. Individuals' information won't be publicly available, but a database of group information, such as the average age of participants, will be public. The goal is that anyone, even nonscientists,

*A research technician in Pittsburgh prepares to collect a blood sample from a participant in the All of Us Research Program. Health data from 1 million volunteers will be compiled in a database for use in studies of the many factors that affect human health.*

will be able to use this database to make discoveries about how age, ethnicity, geographic location, and many other factors influence health. The more people who participate, the more robust and helpful the data will be.

Large, active communities of citizen contributors add to global knowledge in nearly every scientific field, making possible discoveries and advances that simply wouldn't be achievable with smaller data sets. In addition, citizen science inspires and educates the public, boosting citizens' understanding of science as well as their awareness of scientific and environmental issues facing the world. Fred Urquhart says, "One of the great pleasures Norah and I have had in our studies of the monarchs has been receiving letters from children and adults alike, expressing their delight at being introduced to the study of nature through our program of monarch butterfly tagging and research."[28] The success of this project and so many other citizen science projects has made it clear that the opportunity to take part in research can change people's lives. Imani, the young girl who went on her first BioBlitz in 2013, was still actively observing nature three years later. She says, "I was so excited by my first BioBlitz that I now want a future career in the sciences or medicine."[29] Citizen science can propel anyone on a path toward expertise.

"One of the great pleasures Norah and I have had in our studies of the monarchs has been receiving letters from children and adults alike, expressing their delight at being introduced to the study of nature through our program of monarch butterfly tagging and research."[28]

—Fred Urquhart, zoologist at the University of Toronto

# Patterns and Puzzles

Kirill Dudko was just fourteen years old when he saw something no scientist had ever seen before. While sitting at home in Donetsk, Ukraine, he watched a live feed streaming from a camera located almost 3,000 feet (914 m) under the ocean off the coast of Vancouver Island, Canada. Suddenly, a large creature appeared on the screen and devoured a tube-shaped fish. Curious, Dudko emailed the researchers who operated the system of underwater cameras, now a part of Ocean Networks Canada. The group's goal is to monitor the oceans in order to support scientific research. Dudko wrote, "I saw something strange and weird. Some monster just ate a fish in front of me. What was it?"[30]

The researchers had missed the feeding—it had happened in the middle of the night in their time zone. Excited, they reviewed the video, conferred with colleagues, and realized it had been an elephant seal eating a hagfish. It was the first time anyone had ever recorded the event. One of the researchers said that hagfish are too slimy for most predators to eat. Dudko's observation taught the world something new about both species.

Citizen scientists don't have to go out on expeditions to observe the world and collect measurements. They can look for patterns and anomalies (or irregularities) in scientific data from the comfort of their own homes. These citizen scientists are spending their free time looking at pictures, watching videos, playing games, and more, all to help solve scientific problems.

## A Mountain of Data

Thanks to the low cost of high-quality cameras and other sensors and the ease of uploading and storing information

*Canadian researchers were alerted to an unusual sight by a fourteen-year-old citizen scientist in Ukraine. The image he saw on a streaming live feed turned out to be an elephant seal eating a hagfish—something that had never before been recorded.*

online, scientists, researchers, and the citizen scientists who assist them are amassing vast troves of data. Ocean Networks Canada is just one of numerous programs that stream and store live video or capture photos. Meanwhile, other research projects are collecting brain scans, DNA sequences, signals from space, and more. The Kepler space telescope, for instance, recorded the brightness of hundreds of thousands of stars regularly for nine years, generating over 10 billion data points.

Tackling a mountain of data that huge is often an impossibility for a small research team. Professional scientists often don't have the time or resources to watch every video feed, look at every image, or review every measurement that gets collected. "Astronomy is rapidly moving toward the regime where we're going to have more data than we have any hope of manually looking at,"[31] says Chris Beaumont, a software engineer at the

Harvard-Smithsonian Center for Astrophysics. Of course, computer programs help churn through a lot of scientific data, looking for patterns or making calculations. But especially complex models or analyses may require a supercomputer, and getting time on one of these machines is expensive.

## Spare Computer Power

Once again, citizen scientists can come to the rescue. People who don't have the time or ability to track animals, test water, or send in microbe samples can still do their part. They can donate computer time. Thousands of regular computers and mobile devices can provide as much or more processing power than a supercomputer. Programs such as SETI@home recruit volunteers to install software on their computers or devices. That software runs when the device is not in use.

*SETI* stands for "Search for ExtraTerrestrial Intelligence." It's a program that collects and analyzes data from radio telescopes, looking for signals from space that might indicate intelligent life—in other words, aliens. Those signals could come from any point in the vast cosmos. Researchers needed a lot of telescope time and computer power to conduct this search. So in 1999 they designed SETI@home, software that would run as a screensaver on people's desktop computers. The screensaver showed a radio telescope signal and displayed data about the signal. It would detect unusual patterns automatically—users didn't have to do anything. Researchers could then compare anomalies to other observations of the same star or galaxy. "We're kind of hoping that the aliens are sending a constant beacon, and that every time a telescope passes over a point in the sky, we see it,"[32] says Eric Korpela, an astronomer at the University of California, Berkeley, who works on SETI@home.

Much to the researchers' surprise, 1 million people signed up for SETI@home when it launched, and over 4 million people have participated in the program. So far, they haven't found any alien beacons. But they're not done looking. In addition, the researchers' effort to get millions of computers around the world to work on the same problem led to the development of new technology, called the Berkeley Open Infrastructure for Network Computing. It runs all the time, making use of spare computer power without interrupting anything the computer's user is doing. Today many scientists use this platform and others like it to allow volunteers to donate computer time to the scientists' work.

A citizen scientist who wants to donate his or her spare computing power has a huge variety of projects to choose from. Mala riacontrol.net runs through models that simulate how malaria gets transmitted and how the disease might be controlled. Quake-Catcher Network turns computers and devices into seismographs, or tools to detect tremors and earthquakes. To work properly, the computer or device must have an internal accelerometer, a type of sensor common in modern devices. Climateprediction.net uses people's spare computer time to run complex models of global climate. These models try to predict what the earth's climate will be like in the future. A spin-off project, weather@home, runs models for smaller regions. And ATLAS@home runs simulations of particle collisions like the ones that happen inside the Large Hadron Collider, the world's largest scientific machine. These simulations may help lead to new insights in physics. If it's too hard to choose a single project to support, citizen scientists can sign up for World Community Grid, an IBM project that has provided volunteer computer power to a number of different research projects, ranging from solar cell design to cancer research.

## Out of This World

Automatic computer analysis can churn through a lot of data. But computers aren't capable of analyzing everything. When it comes to recognizing certain patterns and anomalies in data, human eyes and minds often do a much better job than computer programs. "There are people who believe that computers are better than people at any task," says Alyssa Goodman, an

*An IBM employee shows a North Carolina college student how the World Community Grid citizen science project will work. Participants provide computer power for projects ranging from solar cell design to cancer research.*

astronomer at Harvard University. "In truth, for nearly all pattern-recognition tasks, evolution has made the human brain very, very good—still better than any computer program."[33] Though artificial intelligence (AI) programs are rapidly improving, people still tend to outperform machines at many tasks, especially ones involving images.

Soon after Kepler launched, a group of astronomers decided that computers alone weren't enough to analyze the billions of data points the space telescope was collecting. Computer programs were looking through the data for obvious signs of exoplanets—planets that orbit stars in other solar systems. These show up as regular dips in a star's brightness, indicating that something has passed in front of it. But computers wouldn't notice anything they hadn't been specifically instructed to look for. So the astronomers set up the citizen science group Planet

Hunters in 2010. "Non-professional astronomers are not looking for one thing . . . they are more alert to little irregularities that are real, but unusual," explains Stella Kafka, an astronomer and director of the American Association of Variable Star Observers, a community of citizen astronomers. "You could call it thousands of untrained eyes, but I call it thousands of open minds."[34]

> "Non-professional astronomers are not looking for one thing. . . . You could call it thousands of untrained eyes, but I call it thousands of open minds."[34]
>
> —Stella Kafka, astronomer and director of the American Association of Variable Star Observers

Adam Szewczyk of Ontario, Canada, was one of those open minds. He went through a short online training session and joined Planet Hunters. After a few months he found something unusual. It was a dip in brightness that didn't look anything like the others. He and a group of other volunteers reached out to professional astronomers, who at first thought it had to be a glitch in the data. "We've seen bad data so many times that it is almost always the reason we see something totally outside of our range of expectations," says Jason Wright, an astronomer at Penn State. But the astronomers came to realize this star was something new and different. "It would not have been spotted without the amateur eyeballs on the data."[35]

Tabetha Boyajian, an astronomer at Louisiana State University, has been studying the unusual star ever since and still doesn't know what is causing the changes in brightness. When Kepler stopped collecting data in 2018, she launched a Kickstarter campaign to crowdfund money for telescope time to keep observing the star. Amateur astronomers also watch it through their backyard telescopes. "I am so excited to see what they'll find,"[36] says Boyajian.

## The Zookeepers

Planet Hunters wasn't the first citizen science project to shake up astronomy. The National Aeronautics and Space Administration

## Community Connections

Some citizen science projects are online only. Participants contribute from their devices, which seems like a solitary activity. Yet through message boards and social media groups dedicated to these projects, participants often form vibrant, close communities. Hanny van Arkel was a Dutch schoolteacher who became famous when she discovered a new type of astronomical object while volunteering for Galaxy Zoo in 2007. It became known as Hanny's Voorwerp (*voorwerp* is the Dutch word for "object"). Though proud of her discovery, van Arkel is most thankful for the friends she's made through participation in the community. "Besides everything I've experienced and learned on this ride, the very best part is the people," she says. Citizen science projects put people around the world in touch with others who share their interests. These people form bonds of friendship that matter just as much as their scientific contributions.

Hanny van Arkel, "A Decade as a Citizen Scientist," *Hanny's Voorwerp* (blog), July 11, 2017. www.hannysvoorwerp.com.

launched the Stardust@home project in 2006 to get help searching through millions of microscope images for tiny specks of dust that stuck to a collector on the *Stardust* spacecraft. And in 2007 a PhD student named Kevin Schawinski faced the daunting task of categorizing 1 million images of galaxies taken during the Sloan Digital Sky Survey. Identifying and classifying galaxy shapes was a task computers couldn't handle. So Schawinski and some colleagues created and launched the website Galaxy Zoo.

Soon people all over the world were classifying seventy thousand images per hour. To help eliminate errors that inexperienced people might introduce, the "Zookeepers," as Schawinski and his cofounders came to be called, had several volunteers look at each image. This type of redundancy is common in a citizen science project. If multiple volunteers' classifications agree, then they are almost certainly correct. Schawinski says, "We had succeeded in creating the world's most powerful pattern-recognising super-computer, and it existed in the linked intelligence of all the people who had logged on to our website: and this global brain was processing this stuff incredibly fast and incredibly accurately. It was extraordinary."[37]

Galaxy Zoo volunteers are still classifying galaxies from new sky surveys. But today that is just one small project out of many on Zooniverse, a website that acts as a home for online citizen science projects of all kinds, from listening to the sounds of tremors in Earthquake Detective to searching for subatomic particles in Higgs Hunters. All of the projects on Zooniverse are web-based. That means participants can complete the task on a computer or device without having to go out into the real world to collect data.

> "We had succeeded in creating the world's most powerful pattern-recognising super-computer, and it existed in the linked intelligence of all the people who had logged on to our website."[37]
>
> —Kevin Schawinski, founder of Galaxy Zoo

## The Birds and the Bees

A huge number of the web-based citizen science projects on Zooniverse and elsewhere involve watching for and identifying animals and plants in images or other data that scientists have already collected. Many projects post photos from camera traps, which are cameras set up to take a picture when a sensor detects motion or heat nearby. In Snapshot Mountain Zebra, people go through these images to identify any animals in the image. In Condor Watch, volunteers help read identification tags on the endangered birds' legs and note how the bird behaves. Other projects use drones or satellites to survey large areas, then get volunteers to help look at the pictures. In Orangutan Nest Watch, people look at drone images for orangutan nests or fig trees, a favorite food source for the primates. In Floating Forests, people look for kelp forests in satellite images of the ocean. Some projects require senses other than vision. In Bat Detective, volunteers listen to audio recordings to pick out which ones are bat calls. Manatee Chat does the same thing for the calls of manatees.

## People Teaching Computers

Scientists often turn to citizen scientists for help when current computer software is unable to recognize images or patterns reliably. However, software's ability to identify objects in images, transcribe handwriting, and perform other pattern-recognition tasks is improving rapidly, thanks to advances in AI software. A lot of AI software in use today works a bit like the human brain—it learns from experience. To teach software how to find faces in photos, researchers fed the program hundreds of thousands of photos with human faces labeled. The more labeled data the AI gets to work with, the better it becomes at finding faces in new photos. This means that citizen science efforts to label images or transcribe handwriting can often be used to improve a computer program's ability to perform the same task. Some citizen scientist programs are taking advantage of this and using volunteers' work to train computer software or even robots. In the game *Astro Drone*, players teach flying robots how to navigate. The games *Phrase Detectives* and *Wordrobe* both help train software to do a better job expressing and understanding human language.

Other projects have historical archives of images or text that they need humans to tag or transcribe in order to make these archives digitally accessible and searchable. In Rainforest Flowers, people look at images from the Field Museum of Natural History's collection and add tags for any fruits, stems, leaves, and colors present in the pictures. Other projects ask people to read and transcribe documents, including scientists' notebooks, letters, research, and more. In Herbaria@home, volunteers transcribe labels on old plant specimens.

## Playing Games

Labeling the shapes of hundreds of galaxies, trying to spot orangutan nests in endless photos of trees, or transcribing ancient botany note cards may get boring after a while. To keep volunteers engaged, some scientists have turned their data sorting and labeling problems into games. *Foldit* was the first citizen science game. The goal is to figure out the most stable shape for a protein. Proteins are molecules that perform many important functions in the body. Each protein forms from a long chain of amino acids. But it is not a straight chain. The chemistry of each link influences the shape. For any chain of amino acids, there are billions of potential shapes but likely only one completely stable shape. Knowing this stable shape reveals how a protein functions. This can help researchers better understand diseases and find new medicines. But they have to puzzle through a dizzying number of possible shapes for every single protein they want to study.

Back in the early 2000s, biochemist David Baker of the University of Washington, Seattle, launched Rosetta@home, a project that borrowed people's spare computer time to methodically go through protein shapes, looking for the best one. (Rosetta@home and a similar project, Folding@home, are both still active). Users could watch the folding action on a screensaver. Some of the users started contacting Baker, explaining that they could see how a protein should fold. So he decided to start a new project that would give volunteers control. The result, *Foldit*, was a game. Claire Baert tried her hand at it in 2015. "Puzzle after puzzle, I was introduced to the different components that make the structure of a protein," she says. "I was unlocking new tools to help me fold my proteins and make them more energy efficient."[38] Baert had been working in the mainstream video game industry, but she soon shifted her focus and founded a website, Citizen Science Games, devoted to science-related games.

> "Puzzle after puzzle, I was introduced to the different components that make the structure of a protein. I was unlocking new tools to help me fold my proteins and make them more energy efficient."[38]
>
> —Claire Baert, founder of Citizen Science Games

## From Mapping the Brain to Fighting Disease

Numerous different games allow citizens to assist scientists and researchers with a range of different problems. Players map out the structure of neurons in the brain in *Eyewire*. This helps researchers understand the brain's connections. In *MalariaSpot*, players look at images of real patients' blood samples to count parasites. This helps doctors diagnose the disease more quickly. In *Fraxinus*, players match colorful gene sequences to help

*This nerve cell and dendrites illustration was generated using 3-D public domain data from* Eyewire, *a citizen science game that maps real neurons. This mapping helps researchers in their studies of the brain.*

researchers fight a disease that is killing ash trees. And in *Stall Catchers*, they look at videos of blood flow in mouse brains to figure out which vessels are flowing and which are stalled. This helps advance Alzheimer's disease research.

The researchers who launched *Stall Catchers* say that it takes their team about a week to do the brain imaging necessary to answer one of their questions about the disease. But finding the stalled blood vessels in those images would take them a year. Having players do that work instead made a huge difference. "We realized that a year's worth of research could be compressed into two weeks,"[39] says Pietro Michelucci, director of the Human Computation Institute, who helped develop the game.

Playing *Sea Hero Quest* also helps Alzheimer's disease research but in a much more abstract way. The main character is an ocean explorer. The game collects data as a player avoids icebergs, volcanoes, and other obstacles; navigates to certain places on a map; and completes other challenges. These data reveal information about people's spatial awareness and how that changes over time. Over 2.5 million people have played the game, and researchers have learned that spatial navigation skills worsen steadily from age nineteen onward. Eventually, a game like this could help diagnose dementia.

"The ingenuity of game players is a formidable force that, if properly directed, can be used to solve a wide range of scientific problems."[40]

—Firas Khatib, biochemist at the University of Washington

These are only a few of the games out there. Thanks to the success of so many of these projects, many scientists and citizens now realize that puzzles and games can do more than provide enjoyment and fill leisure time. They can also unlock new scientific knowledge. In 2011 *Foldit* players figured out a structure that AIDS researchers needed for their work. The problem had stumped scientists for over a decade, but it took the gamers just three weeks to solve it. "The ingenuity of game players is a formidable force that, if properly directed, can be used to solve a wide range of scientific problems,"[40] says Firas Khatib, a biochemist in David Baker's lab at the University of Washington. Even projects that aren't technically games, like hunting for planets or watching live video streams for wildlife, feel fun to people who love space or nature. People who participate in these projects in their free time are enjoying themselves. They're having fun and helping science at the same time.

# Empowering People

The earth shook. Then towering waves traveling at the speed of a jet plane crashed into shore. It was March 11, 2011, and a horrific earthquake and tsunami had hit the northeastern coast of Japan. The disaster killed over fifteen thousand people and damaged or destroyed hundreds of thousands of buildings, including the Fukushima Daiichi Nuclear Power Plant. Joi Ito, a scholar from Japan who studies the ethics of technology, was in the United States interviewing for a job when he got the news. His family and friends back home in Japan were safe. But they were having trouble getting the information they needed from the government about how to stay safe. Everyone knew that radiation had escaped from the power plant. At high levels, radiation can damage living tissue or lead to cancer. Detecting radiation requires a tool called a Geiger counter; however, there weren't enough to go around.

Ito and others weren't willing to wait for help from authorities. They decided to take matters into their own hands. On Twitter, a community of concerned citizens came together. They connected with experts and soon launched a website and organization called Safecast. Hackers in the community came up with a way to build a Geiger counter at home. Soon citizens in Japan were walking around their neighborhoods with these homemade instruments, measuring radiation and reporting the results on Safecast. Almost ten years later, the group is still actively tracking radiation levels and other environmental data in Japan as well as in many other places around the world.

Many citizen science projects, puzzles, and games are hierarchical, or top-down, efforts. They get started because a scientist or institution has a problem to solve that's too big to handle. So the experts recruit and train ordinary people to help. However, sometimes ordinary people see problems or care about issues that scientists and institutions aren't addressing. When these activists band together and use science and engineering to find answers, that's also citizen science. Often, experts and institutions do get involved in these grassroots science efforts, but they're brought in once the regular citizens have already gotten the ball rolling. In the case of Safecast, Ito says, "Over time, more and more of the experts joined this movement. But at the beginning, we absolutely knew nothing. All we had was this kind of desire to figure it out."[41]

"At the beginning, we absolutely knew nothing. All we had was this kind of desire to figure it out."[41]

—Joi Ito, cofounder of Safecast

## In the Wake of Disaster

Disasters are a common precursor to a grassroots scientific data collection effort. In the wake of a horrible natural event or accident, sometimes only the people most closely affected have both the access and motivation to gather and analyze information. In 2010 an explosion on BP's *Deepwater Horizon* oil rig killed eleven people. Oil gushed into the surrounding ocean, the Gulf of Mexico. An estimated 210 million gallons (795 million L) of oil polluted the water during the four months it took to seal off the leak. People who lived along the coast in Louisiana, Mississippi, Alabama, and Florida worried about their beaches and wildlife. People working in the fishing industry in the area faced the prospect of losing their jobs, since oil can contaminate seafood.

Despite the severity of the incident, BP wasn't giving out much information. In fact, the company tried to keep locals and journalists away from the spill. "Right away we knew there was a desperate need for watchdogs, a desperate need to elevate the voices of people on the ground,"[42] says Jeffrey Yoo Warren. At the time, he was a student at the MIT Media Lab who had been working with cartographer Stewart Long on a mapping device. It was basically a cheap digital camera fitted into a clear soda bottle and strapped beneath a weather balloon. As the balloon floated through the air, the camera captured photos of the ground or sea beneath. Warren wrote software that stitches these images together into a map.

Warren and Long reached out to a nonprofit called the Louisiana Bucket Brigade. This citizen science group helps communities located near industrial facilities test for contaminated water or air. Shannon Dosemagen, who worked with the nonprofit, had already been asking locals to collect information about the spill. She, Warren, and Long started training volunteers to map the oil spill from above. The maps they made offered a unique and original view of the disaster—a view that no one else was offering to the public.

Dosemagen, Warren, and Long went on to found the Public Laboratory for Open Technology and Science. This online community provides citizens with resources to carry out their own investigations of environmental concerns. It also offers instructions on how to build monitoring tools such as the balloon mapping device from easily available components. "We can all now be scientists," Dosemagen says. "I'm not a trained scientist. But I've become a community scientist because of the internet, because I can learn, I can share results, I can use science to become active in the decisions that are being made about my community."[43]

Meanwhile, a different citizen science project, Humanitarian OpenStreetMap, has helped emergency response efforts in the wake of dozens of natural disasters, including the 2010 earthquakes in Haiti and Chile, the 2015 earthquake in Nepal, Hurricanes Irma and Maria that hit Puerto Rico and other islands in the Caribbean in 2017, and the dam collapse in Laos in 2018. After a disaster like one of these, emergency responders need to know where to go. Jenelle Eli of the American Red Cross responded to the Nepal earthquake, only to discover that many of the small vil-

*A canine emergency response team searches for survivors after the devastating 2015 earthquake in Nepal. Emergency response efforts in Nepal and elsewhere have been aided by the Humanitarian OpenStreetMap citizen science project.*

lages affected were not well mapped. She says, "In order to know where to get help to people in need, we needed to first put those people on the map and see where they were living."[44] The OpenStreetMap software made that possible. It is a lot like Wikipedia in that it allows anyone, anywhere, to add to or edit the map. Working from satellite imagery of cities or towns, users trace and label buildings, roads, and other features. After a natural disaster or other crisis, Humanitarian OpenStreetMap brings ordinary people together—often at events called mapathons—to quickly update the map for the affected area.

## Science for the Marginalized

Knowledge is power. Citizen science can bring knowledge, and therefore power, to communities that have been overlooked, ignored, or even abused due to racism, classism, and other factors. Groups of low-income people or people of marginalized groups have often been kept ignorant of important issues facing their communities. Nancy J. Meyer, an activist who attended a meeting to organize opposition to a new concrete plant in the Baltimore, Maryland, area, says, "Nobody told them that their home was built on top of a landfill. These become throwaway neighborhoods, occupied by throwaway people. We have to find a way to revitalize these places." A 2015 report from the National Association for the Advancement of Colored People found that 78 percent of African Americans in the United States live within 30 miles (48 km) of a coal-fired power plant, a common source of pollution. Other marginalized communities in the United States, including Latinos, indigenous people, and low-income people, are also more likely to live near highly polluting facilities. Training people in these communities to become citizen scientists gives them a voice and a means to take action.

Quoted in Courtland Milloy, "Citizen Scientists Are the New Community Activists," *Washington Post*, April 10, 2018. www.washingtonpost.com.

## Patient Activists

Some citizen science projects help bring attention to a crisis that authority figures aren't paying enough attention to. People who spearhead these types of projects often see themselves as activists with a mission. They become citizen scientists in service to that mission. People with rare diseases and other medical conditions often fall into this category. They may feel as if the scientific and medical community isn't doing enough for them. In their search for answers, they may become citizen scientists and activists. For example, in 1985, during the early years of the AIDS epidemic, people personally affected by the disease—especially those in the gay community—helped speed up the search for a cure. These activists didn't collect data themselves. But they did help recruit participants for scientific studies and learned enough about the disease to participate in scientific meetings. Today this type of citizen science is often called patient-led research.

Stephen Heywood of Newton, Massachusetts, died of the disease amyotrophic lateral sclerosis (ALS), also known as Lou Gehrig's disease, in 2006. A few years earlier, his two brothers and a friend started the group PatientsLikeMe. The group enables people to share their own health information, including how a disease progresses and what effect any treatments have, in the hopes of finding answers in all of the combined data. In 2008 patients with ALS used the website to organize their own clinical trial of an experimental treatment. Each patient who wanted to try the treatment was matched with someone who didn't so that the trial would have a control group, something that is very important in medical research. The groups Raremark and Findacure also help connect patients with each other and with researchers.

## The Bucket Brigades

Environmental activists often turn to science to support their cause as well. Denny Larson was already a seasoned environmental activist when he founded the group Global Community Monitor, also known as the Bucket Brigade, in 2001. He says what he does is citizen science but that he prefers the term *community-based participatory research*. Larson developed and perfected a method to test air quality in a bucket. The system works like breathing. Larson explains, "The bucket is the body, the bag is the lung, and there's a pump that serves as a diaphragm, bringing in air so it can be sealed and sent to the lab for testing."[45] Larson's group has worked with communities living near industrial complexes and oil and gas production sites around the world. The Louisiana Bucket Brigade that Dosemagen volunteered for is a sister organization that grew out of one of these partnerships.

Another community Larson partnered with is in Durban, South Africa. In the neighborhood of South Durban, many people live alongside an industrial complex that includes chemical manufacturing plants, oil refineries, and hazardous waste dumps. Desmond D'Sa was resettled there as a child under apartheid, a government program that forcibly segregated the country by race. "We were deliberately placed to live alongside dirty industries,"[46] D'Sa says. Though apartheid has ended, many people still live in South Durban. D'Sa watched as people around him got sick. "A seven-year-old child died of leukemia in my neighborhood, and that woke me up,"[47] he says.

He founded the South Durban Community Environmental Alliance to campaign against toxic waste dumping. In the early 2000s the group began working with Larson to use buckets to test the air. "I swear by the bucket because it works,"[48] says D'Sa. His efforts helped lead to the closure in 2011 of a hazardous waste landfill and earned him the Goldman Environmental Prize in 2014.

*Denny Larson (center) helps community activists in central California measure air quality using the bucket method he developed. Larson's Bucket Brigade has partnered with citizen scientists in communities around the world.*

## Inspiring Political Action

In the United States, Bucket Brigades have also inspired political action. Deborah Thomas, a community organizer in Clark, Wyoming, had to evacuate her home in 2006 after a well at a nearby fracking operation blew out. Fracking is a controversial method of getting at oil and gas reserves trapped in rocks deep underground. It involves injecting chemical-filled water to make cracks in shale rock. In a blowout, fracking chemicals may contaminate groundwater. The state kept an eye on water contamination after the incident. But Thomas also worried about the air—it smelled funny. "We started asking the state to monitor it, and of course they wouldn't," she says. "They didn't have any money to do it. And so we decided to do it ourselves."[49] She reached out to Larson and got involved in a study he was working on to assess air quality near oil and gas production sites in five states, Arkansas, Colorado, Ohio, Pennsylvania, and Wyoming.

"We started asking the state to monitor [the air], and of course they wouldn't. They didn't have any money to do it. And so we decided to do it ourselves."[49]

—Deborah Thomas, community organizer in Clark, Wyoming

Scientists, companies, and government agencies often mistrust data gathered by activists. And they have a good reason to. Scientists should conduct their work without any biases or motivation to come to a specific conclusion. "Being able to be seen as a rigorous scientist without bias can be a real challenge [for citizen scientists],"[50] says Ben Duncan of the Multnomah County Health Department in Oregon. People who already believe that contamination is present in their community may deliberately sabotage or accidentally influence the results of an experiment in order to support their beliefs. Larson believes he designed his experiments carefully to avoid these types of problems. With the assistance of David Carpenter, a professional scientist and physician at the Institute for Health & the Environment at the State University of New

York at Albany, the group got their study published in 2014 in a peer-reviewed scientific journal. This was important because it meant independent scientists had reviewed the group's methods and given them a stamp of approval. The study showed that 40 percent of the air samples the group collected had levels of toxic chemicals above what the government considers safe. The study was one of the factors that convinced the state of New York to ban fracking. Larson says that moment was "very gratifying."[51]

## Exposing Injustice

Activists often come together out of fear or concern about something happening to a community. When subjective feelings and experiences get combined with unbiased, scientific data, activism becomes stronger and more effective. "You're both taking the expertise of the academic and overlaying it with the expertise of the community. . . . The community perspective is from the heart, and the science perspective is from the brain,"[52] says Duncan. As a case in point, several groups of indigenous people in Peru complained about frequent oil spills contaminating their environment. But the government and oil companies denied responsibility. So the Achuar, Wampis, and other indigenous peoples connected with the nonprofit organization Amazon Watch and began using GPS locators, cameras, and other equipment to document contamination from oil spills. The scientific evidence the indigenous communities gathered was impossible to ignore.

"The community perspective is from the heart, and the science perspective is from the brain."[52]

—Ben Duncan, Multnomah County Health Department, Oregon

Another example of a community coming together to expose a serious environmental problem happened in Flint, Michigan. It all began when LeeAnne Walters, a stay-at-home parent, noticed that her tap water had turned brown one day in December 2014. She and her family also experienced troubling symptoms,

## The Maker Movement

Alongside the citizen science movement, the maker movement is also gaining momentum. A blend of hackers and artisans, the people of this movement use technology to encourage and inspire people to create rather than consume. At hackathons, makers come together to solve a problem with technology. These events often prompt participants to program an app, build a website, or come up with hardware that will help promote a cause or solve a problem. Zach Kaplan, chief executive officer of an online store for designers in the movement, says, "It has the potential of giving anyone the tools they need to become makers and move them from passive users to active creators." He explains that the costs of tools such as 3-D printers and robotics parts are dropping. In addition, people have easy access to instructions on how to use these tools. Like citizen scientist activists, makers don't wait for others to provide them with answers. They make the technology they want to see in the world.

Quoted in Tim Bajarin, "Why the Maker Movement Is Important to America's Future," *Time*, May 19, 2014. http://time.com.

including hair loss, rashes, and cramping pains. The city tested her water and discovered lead at dangerous levels. But city officials claimed the problem was limited to her home. Walters suspected otherwise. So she spent her free time reading technical documents about the city's water and discovered that treatments to prevent corrosion hadn't been performed. That's when she got in touch with a scientist. He coached her through the process of setting up a rigorous, scientific test of the city's water system. She coordinated the collection of over eight hundred samples from every zip code in the city. This effort led the city to shut down its water system in 2016.

And it inspired people in other communities to organize similar tests. "All we want to know is what's happening in our homes, and if we can independently verify that, there's no reason not to do that,"[53] said Tony Spagnoli, who helped organize Philly Unleaded, a group that's helping residents of Philadelphia, Pennsylvania, test their own water for lead. The group's efforts got the city to update its water-testing methods.

Several programs exist to help citizens who are concerned about the environment test its health for themselves. FreshWater Watch is a program that engages people around the world to test freshwater resources. In Nanjing, China, data that volunteers collected showed that the local government likely wasn't doing enough to improve urban water treatment, says Yuchao

*High school students in New York help a researcher check a net for American eels. The researcher leads citizen science projects that collect data for use by other scientists.*

Zhang, an associate professor at the Nanjing Institute of Geography and Limnology. Other citizen science projects coordinate the collection of air-quality data to help keep tabs on air pollution. In 2018 twenty thousand people in Belgium paid for and installed air-pollution sensors that collected air-quality data for a month. Filip Meysman, a biogeochemist at the University of Antwerp in Belgium, says, "[The project] has given us a data set which it is not possible to get by other means."[54]

In Beijing, China, air pollution is a huge problem. On some days toxic smog covers the city so thickly that children and the elderly are advised to stay indoors. The people who do go out often wear filter masks. But the Chinese government hasn't always been forthcoming with its air-quality data. From 2012 to 2014, the organization Float conducted workshops with Beijing residents to show them how to measure air quality for themselves using sensors attached to kites. Kite flying is a traditional art in China, explains Xiaowei Wang, an American student who helped organize the project. The workshops attracted kite enthusiasts, retirees, parents with children, and residents concerned with or curious about pollution. Wang Youheng, a participant in one of the workshops, is a communications clerk in Beijing. He says, "We're extremely interested in the quality of the air around us."[55] Xiaowei Wang says that the workshop gave people like him a way to turn their interest into action. "As they go through the workshop and we talk to them more about air pollution . . . I think there's a sense of action that starts to happen and you really feel like you can start to change things instead of just seeing the data on TV."[56]

## Changing the World

The people in all of these towns and cities in South Africa, China, Peru, Belgium, and the United States didn't just wait around for the government to send experts or regulators to test their water or air. They did it themselves. Shannon Dosemagen says, "If we don't have data coming from people who are supposedly enforcing and regulating for us—protecting our communities—then we need to figure out how we can take that accountability in our hands."[57] When enough local people become energized and empowered to do something, the government has no choice but to take action.

Citizen science is about people contributing to scientific research. But it has so many other impacts besides adding to human knowledge. Citizen science educates people of all ages, leading some to become professional scientists. It often provides enjoyment as well as a sense of satisfaction or purpose. It helps researchers conquer big data, speeding up medical research and enabling important discoveries. When combined with disaster response and activism, citizen science helps people rebuild or improve their lives. It can also give a voice to impoverished or marginalized communities. It can bring about justice and political action. Citizen science can change the world.

"If we don't have data coming from people who are supposedly enforcing and regulating for us—protecting our communities—then we need to figure out how we can take that accountability in our hands."[57]

—Shannon Dosemagen, cofounder of the Public Laboratory for Open Technology and Science

# Source Notes

### Introduction: Science for Everyone

1. Quoted in Robinson Meyer, "Canadian Amateurs Discovered a New Type of Aurora," *Atlantic*, March 14, 2018. www.theatlantic.com.
2. Quoted in Katherine Xue, "Popular Science," *Harvard Magazine*, January–February 2014. https://harvardmagazine.com.
3. Quoted in Meyer, "Canadian Amateurs Discovered a New Type of Aurora."
4. Caren Cooper, "Citizen Science: Everybody Counts," TEDxGreensboro, May 15, 2017. www.youtube.com/watch?v=G7cQHSqfSzI&feature=youtu.be.

### Chapter One: Unexpected Experts

5. Jon Larsen, interview with the author, December 3, 2018.
6. Quoted in Kathryn Hulick, "On the Lookout for Micro-Missiles from Space," Science News for Students, March 7, 2019. www.sciencenewsforstudents.org.
7. Quoted in Esther Addley, "Interview: The Ascent of One Woman," *Guardian* (Manchester), April 2, 2003. www.theguardian.com.
8. Quoted in Scholastic, "Q & A with Dinosaur Expert Sue Hendrickson," October 17, 2018. www.scholastic.com.
9. Quoted in Virginia Morell, "35 Who Made a Difference: Richard Leakey." *Smithsonian*, November 1, 2005. www.smithsonianmag.com.
10. Quoted in Amber Dance, "Outside Science," Symmetry, March–April 2008. www.symmetrymagazine.org.
11. Quoted in Dance, "Outside Science."
12. Quoted in Sharman Apt Russell, *Diary of a Citizen Scientist: Chasing Tiger Beetles and Other New Ways of Engaging the World*. Corvallis: Oregon State University Press, 2014, p. 25.

13. Quoted in James Vyver, *"Maratus Harrisi*: The Tiny Peacock Spider Discovered by Canberra Man Stuart Harris in Namadgi National Park," ABC News, August 14, 2014. www.abc.net .au.
14. Quoted in Erika Hayasaki, "Kanzius Cancer Machine Gets Its First Human Trial," *Newsweek*, July 21, 2015. www.news week.com.
15. Sharon Terry, "Science Didn't Understand My Kids' Rare Disease Until I Decided to Study it," TED, November 2016. www .ted.com.
16. Quoted in Caren Cooper, *Citizen Science: How Ordinary People Are Changing the Face of Discovery*. New York: Overlook, 2016, p. 24.
17. Loree Griffin Burns, *Citizen Scientists: Be a Part of Scientific Discovery from Your Own Backyard*. New York: Macmillan, 2012, p. 6.
18. Quoted in Lisa Grossman, "8-Year-Olds Publish Scientific Bee Study," *Wired*, December 21, 2010. www.wired.com.
19. Beau Lotto and Amy O'Toole, "Science Is for Everyone, Kids Included," TED, June 2012. www.ted.com.

**Chapter Two: Gathering a Team**

20. Quoted in GrrlScientist, "Join a Global Bird Census in Your Backyard to Celebrate the Year of the Bird," *Forbes*, February 11, 2018. www.forbes.com.
21. Fred Melgert and Carla Hoegen, "Fred Melgert/Carla Hoegen," iNaturalist, January 20, 2018. www.inaturalist.org.
22. Quoted in *National Geographic*, *Imani's BioBlitz*, video, August 21, 2013. www.nationalgeographic.org.
23. Quoted in Cooper, *Citizen Science*, p. 26.
24. Quoted in Alycia Crall, "It's Raining Cats and Dogs and CoCoRaHS Wants to Know Where and How Many Fell," *Citizen Science Salon* (blog), *Discover*, March 11, 2017. http://blogs .discovermagazine.com.

25. Quoted in Sarah Kaplan, "A Potentially Powerful New Antibiotic Is Discovered in Dirt," *Washington Post*, February 13, 2018. www.washingtonpost.com.

26. Quoted in Kristen French, "Inside the Search for New Antibiotics," Medium, November 2, 2017. https://medium.com.

27. Quoted in Heather Buschman, "Big Data from World's Largest Citizen Science Microbiome Project Serves Food for Thought," UC San Diego Health, May 15, 2018. https://health.ucsd.edu.

28. Quoted in Flight of the Butterflies, "The Discovery Story," 2012. www.flightofthebutterflies.com.

29. Quoted in *National Geographic*, "Bioblitz." www.nationalgeographic.org.

## Chapter Three: Patterns and Puzzles

30. Quoted in Radio Free Europe/Radio Liberty, "Ukrainian Teen's 'Monster' Sighting Leads to Unique Undersea Video," January 30, 2013. www.rferl.org.

31. Quoted in Xue, "Popular Science."

32. Quoted in Sarah Scoles, "A Brief History of SETI@Home," *Atlantic*, May 23, 2017. www.theatlantic.com.

33. Quoted in Xue, "Popular Science."

34. Quoted in Kate Becker, "How Citizen Scientists Discovered the Strangest Star in the Galaxy," *NOVA Next*, PBS, January 3, 2018. www.pbs.org.

35. Quoted in Becker, "How Citizen Scientists Discovered the Strangest Star in the Galaxy."

36. Quoted in Guy Raz, "Citizen Science," *TED Radio Hour*, NPR, September 29, 2017. www.npr.org.

37. Quoted in Tim Adams, "Galaxy Zoo and the New Dawn of Citizen Science," *Guardian* (Manchester), March 17, 2012. www.theguardian.com.

38. Quoted in Shayna Keyles, "Citizen Science Games Mix Design with Discovery," *GotScience Magazine*, July 25, 2018. www.gotscience.org.

39. Quoted in *The Crowd & the Cloud*, "Even Big Data Starts Small," PBS, 2017. http://crowdandcloud.org.
40. Quoted in Ed Yong, "Computer Gamers Solve Problem in AIDS Research That Puzzled Scientists for Years," *National Geographic,* September 18, 2011. www.nationalgeographic.com.

## Chapter Four: Empowering People

41. Quoted in Raz, "Citizen Science."
42. Quoted in *The Crowd & the Cloud*, "Even Big Data Starts Small."
43. Shannon Dosemagen, "How the BP Oil Spill Inspired a New Citizen Science Model," Bioneers Annual Conference, 2015. https://bioneers.org.
44. Quoted in *The Crowd & the Cloud*, "Even Big Data Starts Small."
45. Quoted in *The Crowd & the Cloud*, "Free Speech in Citizen Science: Q&A with Denny Larson," Medium, May 16, 2017. https://medium.com.
46. Quoted in Melissa Jane Cook, "D'Sa Lauded for Fight for Environmental Justice," Brand South Africa, May 23, 2014. www.brandsouthafrica.com.
47. Quoted in Beth Gardiner, "Air of Revolution: How Activists and Social Media Scrutinise City Pollution," *Guardian* (Manchester), January 31, 2014. www.theguardian.com.
48. Quoted in Gardiner, "Air of Revolution."
49. Quoted in *The Crowd & the Cloud*, "Citizens + Scientists," PBS, 2017. http://crowdandcloud.org.
50. Quoted in Dalal Kheder et al., "How Activism Drives Citizen Science," *Tyee*, April 26, 2013. https://thetyee.ca.
51. Quoted in *The Crowd & the Cloud*, "Free Speech in Citizen Science."
52. Quoted in Kheder et al., "How Activism Drives Citizen Science."

53. Quoted in Jared Bray, "The No-Bullshit Guide to How Phil-adelphia Tests for Lead in Its Drinking Water," *Philadelphia*, June 8, 2016. www.phillymag.com.

54. Quoted in Aisling Irwin, "No PhDs Needed: How Citizen Science Is Transforming Research," *Nature*, October 23, 2018. www.nature.com.

55. Quoted in Derek Mead, "Monitoring Beijing's Air Quality Is as Easy as Flying a Kite," Motherboard, May 13, 2013. https://motherboard.vice.com.

56. Quoted in BBC, "Beijing Pollution Monitored with Kite-Mounted Sensors," August 24, 2012. www.bbc.com.

57. Quoted in Emmalina Glinskis, "Meet the Community Scientists Shaping the New Environmental Resistance," *Nation*, July 19, 2018. www.thenation.com.

# Find a Citizen Science Project

New citizen science projects are launching all the time. And on-going projects run regular events. Below are a few of the web-sites that help connect people to citizen science projects. Other sources worth checking include NASA, *National Geographic*, and *Scientific American*.

## Play Games to Help Science

**Citizen Science Games** (https://citizensciencegames .com). This website keeps an updated list of citizen sci-ence games. It also posts articles and interviews about the intersection between the worlds of science and gaming.

## Make Your Own Project

**CitSci** (www.citsci.org). This website makes it easy for professional or amateur researchers to create their own citizen science projects, recruit volunteers, and collect and analyze data. It also helps connect people to ongo-ing projects of all kinds.

## Join Interactive Science Labs

**NOVA Labs** (www.pbs.org/wgbh/nova/labs). NOVA Labs offers a range of interactive labs and games that educate students and also engage people in scientific discovery.

### Find the Perfect Project Near You

**SciStarter** (https://scistarter.com). The Project Finder on this website lets people search for citizen science projects in a particular area or on a certain topic. Projects can also be filtered by type (such as online-only or an outdoor walk).

### Take Surveys and Join Experiments

**Volunteer Science** (https://volunteerscience.com). This is an online laboratory in which people can take surveys and participate as subjects in online experiments. The website makes it easier for social and behavioral researchers to connect with people willing to become active participants in their research.

### Contribute Instantly to Online Projects

**Zooniverse** (www.zooniverse.org). The projects on Zooniverse are online-only and created by professional researchers. Clicking or tapping on a project opens it up. After a quick tutorial, volunteers can get started. They can spend as much or as little time as they want on each project.

# Organizations to Contact

**Citizen Science Alliance**
website: www.citizensciencealliance.org

The Citizen Science Alliance is a group of scientists, software developers, and educators who work together to manage the online-only citizen science projects on the Zooniverse website.

**Citizen Science Association**
website: www.citizenscience.org

The Citizen Science Association runs the annual CitSci conference, which brings together leaders and learners from the citizen science community. The association also publishes an open-access, peer-reviewed scientific journal, *Citizen Science: Theory and Practice*, that covers research about citizen science.

**European Citizen Science Association (ECSA)**
website: https://ecsa.citizen-science.net

The ECSA is a nonprofit organization that supports the citizen science movement in Europe by helping projects get off the ground and performing research about citizen science. The organization also runs an online Citizen Science challenge for European students to help them get involved.

**Extreme Citizen Science (ExCiteS)**
website: www.geog.ucl.ac.uk/research/research-centres /excites

This research group at University College London works to enable communities to start their own citizen science projects to address local environmental issues. The project aims to include any user, regardless of his or her cultural background or literacy level.

## Human Computation Institute
website: http://humancomputation.org

The Human Computation Institute is a nonprofit organization that aims to tackle societal problems with the power of crowds.

## iNaturalist
website: www.inaturalist.org

This online community is a joint venture by the California Academy of Sciences and the National Geographic Society. It helps people identify plants and animals. People can participate on a computer or mobile device. The photos and identifications that people share provide important data to researchers.

## Public Lab
website: https://publiclab.org

Public Lab is an online community and nonprofit organization. Its goal is to democratize science and bring people together to address environmental problems. The community has a special focus on the development of monitoring tools that anyone can build and use.

# For More Information

## Books

Loree Griffin Burns, *Citizen Scientists: Be a Part of Scientific Discovery from Your Own Backyard*. New York: Macmillan, 2012.

Caren Cooper, *Citizen Science: How Ordinary People Are Changing the Face of Discovery*. New York: Overlook, 2016.

Mary Ellen Hannibal, *Citizen Scientist: Searching for Heroes and Hope in an Age of Extinction*. New York: Experiment, 2016.

Susanne Hecker et al., eds., *Citizen Science: Innovation in Open Science, Society and Policy*. London: UCL, 2018.

Greg Landgraf, *Citizen Science: Guide for Families: Taking Part in Real Science*. Chicago: Huron Street, 2013.

## Internet Sources

*The Crowd and the Cloud*, directed by Geoffrey Haines-Stiles, PBS, 2017. http://crowdandcloud.org.

Aisling Irwin, "No PhDs Needed: How Citizen Science Is Transforming Research," *Nature*, October 23, 2018. www.nature.com.

Dalal Kheder et al., "How Activism Drives Citizen Science," *Tyee*, April 26, 2013. https://thetyee.ca.

Courtland Milloy, "Citizen Scientists Are the New Community Activists," *Washington Post*, April 10, 2018. www.washingtonpost.com.

Guy Raz, "Citizen Science," *TED Radio Hour*, NPR, September 29, 2017. www.npr.org.

Jack Stilgoe, "Is Citizen Science the Future of Research or a Recipe for Bad Science?," *Guardian* (Manchester), November 8, 2016. www.theguardian.com.

Kathrine Xue, "Popular Science," *Harvard Magazine*, January–February 2014. https://harvardmagazine.com.

# Index

# Picture Credits

# About the Author

Kathryn Hulick got into citizen science in college, when she put her computer to work searching for aliens with SETI@ home (she didn't find any). Later, she classified galaxies for Galaxy Zoo. But her biggest adventure was serving two years in the Peace Corps in Kyrgyzstan, teaching English. She did not have a cell phone and had to travel for half an hour by taxi to use the Internet. But after her return to the United States, she embraced digital technology and began writing books and articles for kids. Her books include *Careers in Robotics*, *How Robotics Is Changing the World*, and *Robotics and Medicine*. She also contributes regularly to *Muse* magazine and the Science News for Students website. Her current favorite citizen science project involves labeling pictures of flowers. She lives in Massachusetts with her husband and son.